A B C D E F G H I J K L M N O P

THE STORY BEHIND
HALLOWEEN

MELISSA RAÈ SHOFNER

PowerKiDS press

New York

Published in 2020 by The Rosen Publishing Group, Inc.
29 East 21st Street, New York, NY 10010

First Edition

Editor: Tanya Dellaccio
Book Design: Reann Nye

Photo Credits: Cover, p. 1 Rawpixel.com/Shutterstock.com; pp. 4, 6, 8, 12, 14, 16, 18, 20, 22 Preto Perola/Shutterstock.com; p. 5 Ariel Skelley/DigitalVision/Getty Images; p. 7 Matt Cardy/Getty Images News/Getty Images; p. 9 Hulton Archive/Getty Images; p. 11 Sean Locke Photography/Shutterstock.com; p. 13 Rainier Ampongan/Shutterstock.com; p. 15 Bill Chizek/Shutterstock.com; p. 17 ullstein bild/Getty Images; p. 19 Sergey Novikov/Shutterstock.com; p. 21 Monkey Business Images/Shutterstock.com; p. 22 YanLev/Shutterstock.com.

Library of Congress Cataloging-in-Publication Data

Names: Shofner, Melissa Raé, author.
Title: The story behind Halloween / Melissa Raé Shofner.
Description: New York : PowerKids Press, [2020] | Series: Holiday histories |
  Includes webography. | Includes index.
Identifiers: LCCN 2018060238| ISBN 9781725300484 (paperback) | ISBN
  9781725300507 (library bound) | ISBN 9781725300491 (6 pack)
Subjects: LCSH: Halloween–Juvenile literature.
Classification: LCC GT4965 .S52 2020 | DDC 394.2646–dc23
LC record available at https://lccn.loc.gov/2018060238

Manufactured in the United States of America

CPSIA Compliance Information: Batch #CSPK19. For Further Information contact Rosen Publishing, New York, New York at 1-800-237-9932.

CONTENTS

Trick or Treat!. 4

A Spooky Start 6

More to the Mix 10

All Saints' Day 12

Coming to America 16

Costumes and Candy 18

Happy Halloween! 22

Glossary 23

Index 24

Websites 24

Trick or Treat!

Halloween is **celebrated** each year on October 31. In the United States, Canada, and many European countries, children dress up in **costumes** and go trick-or-treating. Some children wear silly costumes. Others wear spooky costumes. No matter what you wear, everyone gets candy!

A Spooky Start

Halloween **traditions** are very old. Around 2,000 years ago, people in Britain and Ireland celebrated Samhain (SOW-win). Samhain was celebrated on November 1—the beginning of the **Celtic** new year. This day marked the end of summer and the beginning of winter.

The Celts believed the **souls** of the dead visited them during Samhain. Those who had recently died were thought to travel to the afterlife. People lit large fires to scare away bad spirits. Some people wore masks to hide from evil spirits.

More to the Mix

By AD 43, the Romans had taken over most Celtic lands. Two Roman holidays mixed with Samhain. On Feralia, in late October, the Romans celebrated their dead. Another day honored Pomona, the goddess of fruit trees. The tradition of bobbing for apples may come from this day.

All Saints' Day

All **Saints**' Day is the day Christians celebrate saints of the church. It's celebrated on November 1. In AD 1000, November 2 became known as All Souls' Day, which honored family and friends who had died. All Souls' Day was much like Samhain.

People began to call the night before All Saints' Day—October 31—All Hallows' Eve. "Hallow" used to be another word for "saint." The traditions of Samhain and All Hallows' Eve mixed to help form the holiday we know today as Halloween. Some traditions have changed over time.

Coming to America

At first, not many people in America celebrated Halloween. Some people celebrated the **harvest** by singing, dancing, and telling ghost stories. Still, Halloween was banned by some **religions**. The holiday became more common in the mid-19th century as more Europeans began moving to the United States.

Costumes and Candy

On Halloween today, many children dress up in costumes and go door to door asking for candy. It's possible that this tradition came from an old All Souls' Day tradition of giving people treats called "soul cakes."

People used to play tricks such as letting farm animals loose on Halloween. Today, the words "trick or treat" come from this old practice. The idea is that if the person doesn't give out a treat, others will play a trick on them.

Happy Halloween!

Jack-o'-lanterns are another common Halloween tradition. Long ago, people **carved** scary faces into vegetables called turnips. Today, we use pumpkins. Will you trick-or-treat and carve a jack-o'-lantern this year? It's never too early to start planning your costume!

GLOSSARY

carve: To cut a picture into a surface or to cut something into a shape.

celebrate: To do something special or enjoyable for an important event or holiday.

Celtic: Of or relating to the Celts, a group of people who lived long ago in the Britain Isles and parts of western Europe.

costume: The clothes that are worn by someone who is trying to look like a different person or thing.

harvest: To gather crops after they've grown. Also, the crop itself.

religion: The belief in a god or a group of gods.

saint: A person who is honored by the church.

soul: The spiritual part of a person that is believed to give life to the body and that in many religions is believed to live forever.

tradition: A way of thinking, behaving, or doing something that's been used by people in a particular society for a long time.

INDEX

A
All Hallow's Eve, 14
All Saints' Day, 12, 14
All Souls' Day, 12, 18

B
Britain, 6

C
Canada, 4
Celts, 8
Christians, 12

F
Feralia, 10

I
Ireland, 6

P
Pomona, 10

R
Romans, 10

S
Samhain, 6, 8, 10, 12, 14

U
United States, 4, 16

WEBSITES

Due to the changing nature of Internet links, PowerKids Press has developed an online list of websites related to the subject of this book. This site is updated regularly. Please use this link to access the list: www.powerkidslinks.com/HH/halloween